ABOVE
AVERAGE

Discovering the Gift of Intercession

TIFFANY J. MARSHALL

ISBN: 979-8-9867000-8-3

For permission requests, contact the publisher.

Extreme Overflow Publishing

A Brand of Extreme Overflow Enterprises, Inc

P.O. Box 1811, Dacula, GA 30019

www.extremeoverflow.com

Send feedback to info@extremeoverflow.com

Printed in the United States of America

Library of Congress Catalog in-Publication

Data is available for this title.

Dedication

This book is dedicated to my mother, Clarissa J Marshall for always being my rock. Sometimes no questions are even asked. Nothing even has to be said. She just does, and I'm so grateful for her love for me, my girls and mostly her love for God. I love love and appreciate you so very much Ma. Many God continue to pour out His blessings over your life.

To my daughters Tyanna Young / my heart, Kayla Young / my soul, and Jessica Young /my joy, everything I do is for you three. You make me second-guess everything. You unstoppable young woman of God don't realize how much you really mean to me and how you're going impact this world, my lion cubs forever.

To my brother Michael Black, I truly appreciate everything you ever done for me. Life hasn't always been easy, but we made it and I thank you for always being there for me as my big brother.

To my Transparency Group: Although you all entered my life in different stages of my journey you all have always been there for me no matter what. We laughed, cried and prayed together. I thank you all for keeping me grounded and allowing me to be myself in a judgement free zone. I love you all in different ways and I so proud of how far God has brought you and the work that He's doing in your lives. Thank you for being my friend. Dr. Nancy Brown Willis, Dan-ia Chambers, Robin McCatty, Clarence Rowell Jr. and VerNece Smith.

To my Push Section: Pastors Jason and Sharae LaPlanche. My pastors, my leaders, my friends: Thank you so much for your obedience to God and seeing me for who God created me to be. Your love, wisdom, and guidance is unmatched. Thank you for creating a space that I can comfortably walk in my freedom and allow God's light to shine through me. We started from the bottom and now WE ARE HERE! God be the glory. This is only the beginning.

To Pastor DiAnna Webster-Armstrong Psy.D. Thank you, Thank you, Thank you! I know God sent you back for me. You've helped me through so much mentally, spiritually and naturally words can't even describe. Your love and obedience is 2nd to none and I truly appreciate you for your mentorship, guidance and love.

To my Village: cousin Naeemah Smith, niece Candice Fitzpatrick, friend Carrie Christian, my Motivation family and all of my family and friends. I love you all and I pray that God will draw you closer to Him and allow you to see all that He has in store for you in your life.

May God bless, keep and cover you and your families in Jesus name, AMEN.

Contents

Introduction

Welcome, reader; I'm so honored that you have decided to embark on life's journey with me. It has been such a humbling experience just to be able to write this book. I pray that these stories, testimonials, trials, and adventures may be able to help you on your spiritual walk in some way. In the text, I want you to understand that sharing your testimonies with others can help them overcome the situations and fears they may face. Whether big or small, it can give someone else the courage to move to their next place in God. As you read this book, I pray you will be encouraged, find healing, see things with a new mindset, and learn to trust the God in you and trust God through your process.

> *"And they overcame him by the blood of the Lamb, and by the word of their testimony; and they loved not their lives unto the death."*
> *Revelation 12:11 KJV*

I believe that one scripture can hit you differently depending on the season of life you're in at that moment. As I write this book here are the three of scriptures that have really helped me through this process.

> *"Jesus looked at him and said, "with men this is impossible, but with God all things are possible." Matthew 19:26 NIV*
>
> *"He replied, "because you have so little faith. Truly I tell you, if you have faith as small as a mustard seed, you can say to this mountain, move from here to there, and it will move. Nothing is impossible for you." Matthew 17:20 NIV*
>
> *"But blessed is the one who trusts in the LORD, whose confidence is in him. They will be like a tree planted by the water that sends out its roots by the stream. It does not fear when heat comes; its leaves are always green. It has no worries in a year of drought and never fails to bear fruit." Jeremiah 17:7-8 NIV*

These scriptures remind me that no matter where we are or what we've been through, God will always be there and never fail us. God's unfailing love has been the only thing that has kept me through marriage, divorce, depression, bad habits, addiction, low self-esteem, homelessness, unforgiveness, and many other things. If I did not have God with me, I would not be able to walk or stand in my freedom today. I'm so grateful that God has been more faithful to me than I have been to Him or myself.

> *"We are called to be faithful, not successful. When you are faithful, God will call successful people to follow you." - Pastor Jason LaPlanche*

1

"A letter to Dad"

"You will keep in perfect peace those whose minds are steadfast, because they trust in you. Isaiah 26:3" NIV

You were my first best friend. We did everything together. Going to the gym, working on cars, laughing at you and my brother having a pie-eating contest on Thanksgiving. You were such a joy to be around. When you walked into the room, everybody knew who you were, and I was proud to say that's my dad. As I reminisce over the chain of events nine months before your death, I would never have begun to think that this would be the stepping stone of my ministry. And at that moment, God was setting me up for life events.

You weren't just my Superman; you were everyone's Superman. I rarely saw you get mad. You were full of laughter, and nobody could top your muscle mass, but that disease called Cancer came to destroy you and was determined to take you out. It was indeed your Kryptonite.

Kryptonite is a fictional material that appears primarily in Superman stories published by DC Comics. In its best-known form, it is a green, crystalline material originating from Superman's home world of Krypton. It emits a unique, poisonous radiation that can weaken and kill Kryptonians. But before it could, you gave your life to God, which made a lifelong impression on me. I watched you try everything for relief, and when everything failed, God was the only thing that kept you in perfect peace. At the age of 10, so many things were confusing for me, trying to understand why you were sick, not getting better, and watching my mother fake like she was happy while her heart was slowly breaking. I can still hear her say to you daily, have faith, and God will make a way. These moments started a foundation in me—learning to seek God on my own in private, even as a child. Life has not been easy without you, but we have made it through with God. Your death has taught me to live happily and with no regrets. Don't worry about the small stuff because tomorrow's not a promise but hold on to my faith, no matter the issue. I love you and Thank You, Daddy. You will forever be in my heart.

If you have lost a loved one, I encourage you to write a letter to them and let them know how their death has impacted your life, both negatively and positively. It's time to free yourself. You have to be able to live your life, not just be alive. They would want that for you. Missing them will never go away, but acceptance helps the process.

2

First Encounters

What is an intercessor?

Wikipedia defines an intercessor as a person who intervenes on behalf of another, especially by prayer. Intercessory prayer is the act of praying to a deity on behalf of others or asking a saint in heaven to pray on behalf of oneself or for others. The Apostle Paul's exhortation to Timothy further specifies that prayers of intercession should be made on behalf of all people.

There are times when God will put a person in your heart. That person could be saved or unsaved, but it's your duty as an intercessor to pray on behalf of that person. This is not a small task and does not happen by accident. God has entrusted you with someone's soul to pray for, and you must be obedient. As an intercessor, you are the middleman between God and that other person.

> "I urge you, first of all, to pray for all people. Ask God to help them; intercede on their behalf, and give thanks for them. Pray this way for kings and all who are in authority so that we can live peaceful and quiet lives marked by godliness and dignity. This is good and pleases God our Savior, who wants everyone to be saved and to understand the truth." 1 Timothy 2:1-4 NLT

Per the scripture, we must pray for all people. God has no respect of persons. The same way we are to pray for a king is the same way we need to pray for someone on the street.

I remember my first spiritual encounter as an intercessor when my family and I went to see a Tarot Cards Reader. What are those, you may ask? Tarot cards are small, paper cards that come in a deck, similar to playing cards, and are used for divinatory purposes. Not any saved people should tap into it. I had no idea what that meant, but my daddy's friend told him to try it. At this point, he was desperate for answers about getting rid of his cancer. So, he persuaded my mother to visit them. As we all sat there and the lady kept trying to read the cards, she looked at my mother and said, "something's wrong." She paused and said, "I'm sorry, but the little girl needs to leave because she's blocking my reading for some reason. I can't get through with her sitting here." So my brother took me to sit in the hall while the reader and my parents stayed inside. It wasn't as apparent then, but now I know that the light inside me (God's light) as a child was more substantial than whatever divinatory spirit she was tapping into.

> *14 Don't team up with those who are unbelievers. How can righteousness be a partner with wickedness? How can light live with darkness? 15 What harmony can there be between Christ and the devil? How can a believer be a partner with an unbeliever? 16 And what union can there be between God's temple and idols? For we are the temple of the living God. As God said: "I will live in them and walk among them. I will be their God, and they will be my people.*
>
> *17 Therefore, come out from among unbelievers, and separate yourselves from them, says the LORD. Don't touch their filthy things, and I will welcome you.18 And I will be your Father and you will be my sons and daughters, says the LORD Almighty." 2 Corinthians 6:14-18 NLT*

I recall my second encounter happening when I was nine years old. We were going to drop my brother off at a military college in Missouri. Unaware at the time, my brother heard rumors about the school. Years prior, there were a number of killing and satanic groups on campus. The story has It that there was one part of the school no one was allowed to go in because of the history of crazy things that went on up there. The day after we arrived, we went on a campus tour with one of the older faculty members to learn about the school, the facility, and the campus.

We stood by a building on the left and watched the courtyard as we walked. I remember looking up at the top-floor window and could see someone looking down at me. I said to my mother, "Ma, do you see that person staring at me?" She told me, "Where? I don't see anyone." I said to her, "Right there in the window on the top floor. Look, there she goes again." The instructor turned to me and said, "What are you talking about?" I told him, "There's a girl on that top floor, and she keeps looking at me through the window." He said, "You must be mistaken because that part of the school is closed to everyone." Even at nine years old, I knew what I saw. She looked unfortunate, miserable, and afraid like she wanted to go home and couldn't.

We kept walking around the campus, and by the time we returned to that spot, I looked out the window and didn't see her anymore. I said to myself, "Wait a minute. Maybe there wasn't anyone there." I looked up one last time, and there she was. I saw her look at me, and this time she waved.

I told my mother, "I know what I'm talking about. There she is." The instructor told me, "You may not be seeing a living person, but maybe you're seeing a ghost." We all looked at him like he was crazy. Then he began to tell us about the horrible stories of things that happened on that top floor. He also said, "...sometimes at night, people say they can still hear the screaming and crying of the students that were being tortured up there, and if you look through the window at the top of the staircase when the moon is complete, you can see the silhouette of the girl that was hung in the hallway on the wall. They said there was so much blood that it was too hard to clean, so they painted over it. A few months later, my brother came home.

My third encounter was the day that my father passed. I remember us going to the hospital that day. I knew something was wrong. On the car ride over, my mother and my brother were silent. No one spoke. The radio wasn't playing, and my mind was racing. Every thought imaginable went through my head. When we arrived, I remember sitting in the hallway and could hear my mother cry. It was like I could feel her pain every time she cried. The only thing I knew to do was pray. "Lord, help my mom. Please help my mom. She's hurting, God. Please help her." I watched her strength emerge even though I knew she was sad. After all, I'd seen, it was at this moment that I knew my prayers were answered. Mom was strong in a time she should have fallen apart. She had birthed an intercessor.

3

"The process of Separation"

S o, my one-on-ones with God began when I was 11 years old. I fell very sick with not 1 but 3 rare diseases and was hospitalized for a few weeks. The doctors had no idea what to do with me and weren't sure if I would pull through. My immune system was deficient, and it didn't help that I went through a major depression after my father's passing. I was highly contagious and had to be alone in a room alone.

My mother and brother had to work, but they would come to visit me every day after. Before seeing me, they had to dress like some people visiting another planet for their protection. That just made me more depressed. I had just lost my dad, and now I was in the hospital, and I couldn't even hug my mom because she could get what I had. This was just too much. My body was in so much pain emotionally and physically, and I just wanted my mother to hold me. I found myself talking to God every day, every moment, every time I could because everyone else had a time limit with me. I asked him, "why is this happening to me?".

When playing video games, I would tell Him, "watch me beat this level," or "God, I just want my mom." He was always and never left my side. As I remember this story, this was when God had to separate me from everyone I loved so I could start to build a relationship with Him for myself. I had to learn to trust Him, and He would bring me through a life crisis.

Never underestimate what God can do through a child. He may be starting to build a relationship with a child you know. Help them learn about God, pour into them all you know about their lives, talk to them about god daily, teach them how to pray, and ask them questions about God and what they think. Get their mind and spirits going. You don't know how much your support could help their foundation. I had many years of my parents, grandmother, great-aunt, and aunts, who poured God into me differently. So, when I had nobody in the hospital with me, I knew if I called on God, He would be there.

4

"Set on fire"

One of my favorite movies, *Dirty Dancing,* came out in 1987. I was only five years old. I've been dancing since, and I've always wanted to perform like Patrick Swayze, and Jennifer Grey did in the movie. But there was one scene where the main character was in the corner because the gift that she had her parents didn't want to be displayed, and her co-star said, "Nobody puts Baby in a corner." I've always empathized with that part of the movie because I often felt put in a corner. Kids to adults laughed at me because I was either too tall or skinny, needed to lose weight, made fun of me for being dyslexic and having problems reading, or developed postpartum depression after childbirth, to be quiet because you're too loud. I never seem to fit in anywhere. I always tend to feel like I'm in a corner by myself. I've been used to being the life of the party but feeling alone in the room. For years I allowed what people said about me and to me to keep me in a corner until I started going to church and my one on one's with God began.

I started going to church with my best friend then, and I liked it. As a teenager, she was very active in the church and would ask me to youth service and events. Most of the time, I just went to support her but never wanted to get involved. I felt God wanted to use me somehow but didn't know with what or which way. So I just chilled, watched, and talked to Him like always.

I will never forget the day I gave my life to Christ and got baptized. I was 15 years old. After replaying it repeatedly, all the minor details made up the bigger picture. I simultaneously felt nervous, excited, and overwhelmed as I stepped into the water. My Pastor, Rev. Gerald E. Bell, former pastor of Southern Baptist church in Roxbury, Ma assured me I would be just fine. As I went down and came up, I felt a surge of energy through my body and a burning sensation in the pit of my chest and stomach. To the point where I couldn't catch my breath for a second. Like if something almost knocked the wind out of me. I looked at Rev. Bell, who looked at me with tears in his eyes and said, "You will not be in this ministry for long. God has great things in store for you, and I release you to go when the time comes." I rehearsed that in my head so many times. He saw God in me before I even knew that God was there. That was the first time I felt the Holy Spirit inside of me. My flame was lit at that moment. Now, I just needed to be around people that would help me increase my fire.

I wanted to know more about God, and my Pastor knew I would have to find a new home church. For years I wondered what God showed him on that day, but I knew he gave me what I needed at the time to jump-start my spiritual journey.

"But if I say I'll never mention the LORD or speak in His name, his word burns in my heart like a fire. It's like a fire in my bones! I am worn out trying to hold it in! I can't do it!"

Jeremiah 20:9

5

"The Eye Opener"

"God saved you by his grace when you believed.
And you can't take credit for this; it is a gift from
God. Salvation is not a reward for the good things
we have done, so none of us can boast about it."
Ephesians 2:8-9 NLT

I've always known that there was more to God than I knew. After visiting a few Pentecostal churches with some of my friends from school, it opened my eyes to something new that I wasn't used to seeing the Baptist church in which I started my journey. My boyfriend at the time would say things like, "Ok, let's see which church is better." So I came to visit his church. Even though I've been to a few Pentecostal churches before, this one hit a lot differently. The Pastor, Bishop PW Reed of Total Deliverance International Ministries in

Hyde Park, MA, then called me up to the front and told me that he wanted to pray for me and that God had a word for me. He began to speak something in my spirit that only me and God know.

I thought, OK, this man is hearing from God! This is where I need to be. I went a few more times to ensure I followed God's guidance. At 17 years old, I called my Pastor and told him we needed to talk. Before I visited any other ministry, I sought his approval. In this meeting, I told him everything happening in that church in Hyde Park, and I felt like someone unlocked something inside of me. He said, "Do you remember when you got baptized? I told you that your time was short here. I believe in everything that ministry does, but Southern is not ready for that yet. You, my daughter, have my blessing. Go and allow God to use your life."

Now, being in a Pentecostal ministry, I'm learning about the fruits of the spirit, seeing miracles, signs, and wonders, Witnessing and participating in deliverance services, and empowering in a new way in my Christian walk.

> "Therefore, my dear friends, as you have always obeyed—not only in my presence, but now much more in my absence—continue to work out your salvation with fear and trembling." Philippians 2:12 NIV

6

"Be Great"

After my divorce, I wanted to take a little break from ministry. Not only was my spirit hurt, but my self-esteem was low. At the time, I was teaching dance fitness at my job, and one of my basketball Coaches, Jessica Cabrera a.k.a. JC, saw me getting out of class and said: "Hey, what's up? What's wrong?" Without going into full detail, I said, "I'm tired of my weight. My body has hit a plateau, and dancing just isn't doing it for me anymore." She said how about you join me on the line. I told her I had no idea what you are saying. She began to tell me about Boston having a women's tackle football team. I knew nothing about playing football. I've dated a few football players and love watching football on TV. My brother played football his entire life. So, it's always been around me, but I knew nothing about playing it for myself. She said just come out, and we'll teach you. I took her up on that offer. It was one of the best decisions I could have ever made that season. It pushed me to levels that I never knew I could physically do. I wasn't the best player on the line, but I got in and out of it more than just a workout.

My purpose is more significant than me. I was a member of this team, and I know that God planted me here for a reason. Women that I probably would have never met I was able to talk to, learn their stories, pray with, and pray for them. Have God conversations with some who have never been to church or would never return to it. When one of our players got severely injured and had to be taken away in the ambulance, I walked up to her as she was unconscious and prayed. I knew I needed to intercede on her behalf. I didn't care that I was in full uniform or the middle of a football field. I know she needed prayer. When I finished praying, I saw both teams holding hands and praying together. The power of prayer can bring people together. I believe that football is where I found my strength as an intercessor. It gave me physical resilience. I was learning to be prepared for the front line—being able to push anything in front of me. Having my physical body match up with my spiritual being put me in a different position as an intercessor. I uplifted my physical man to withstand spiritual warfare. Wikipedia says that

Spiritual warfare is the Christian concept of fighting against the work of preternatural evil forces. Based on the biblical belief in evil spirits.

In football, I got mentally and physically challenged. I've built great relationships, found a new sense of purpose, learned to coach football, became an even better role model for young girls, and met some fantastic, phenomenal women from all different nationalities and backgrounds. I couldn't be more grateful to JC and the Boston Renegades family. I went from being a Zumba dance fitness instructor to a four-time National Women's football Champion. In a documentary movie written about the team and I was able to ride on the Patriots airplane and was able to sign our team's football in the Football Hall of Fame in Canton, Ohio. Wow!

"I make known the end from the beginning, from ancient times, what is still to come. I say, 'My purpose will stand, and I will do all that I please.' From the east, I summon a bird of prey; from a far-off land, a man to fulfill my purpose. What I have said, that I will bring about; what I have planned, that I will do." Isaiah 46:10-11 NIV

7

"Motivate Everything"

It's so funny how you meet people and never think that it would turn into anything, but one thing I know is that God will always align people with like-mindedness and purpose. After stepping away from the church experience for a few years, it was time to go back and look for a new church home. I went through several churches in the city of Boston and around. Everywhere I went, I just didn't fit. I was looking for balance. Even though people say there is no perfect balance and no perfect church, I was looking for the balance I needed. I was looking for somewhere I could fit in, see myself and grow, and no one knew who I was but wanted to get to know me for the God inside of me, not to whom I was connected. I wanted to be in a place where no one knew my name. I'm a worshiper, Intercessor and I love to worship God. I love to sing and dance. That's my thing, that's who I am, and I know God has put me on this Earth to make a loud noise. I needed to be where I could be my authentic self and not have to change to fit in or look funny because you could hear my voice in the back.

God gave me a vision when I was in my old ministry. While on the altar giving announcements one day, I saw myself in a glass box. Every time I tried to raise my arms, the container was so tight that I could not extend my arms. Every time I tried to move my legs, I could only hold them straight. At that moment, I knew that my season was up there and a shift was about to occur. I stopped for a moment, prayed, and continued with the church announcements. That Sunday, when I got home, I began to write to my pastor to tell him I was stepping down from all of my responsibilities in the ministry. I told him it was time for me to look for a new home church. My oldest daughter and I were leaving. I knew the ministry was no longer for us, and it was time to go. 5 years later, I bumped into an old friend from middle school. We exchanged numbers, and she did my hair. So, I made an appointment with her. That was the start of our reconnecting. I talked about my church experience as she talked about hers. We had a lot of things in common. I told her I teach dance fitness, and she offered to come to teach at her church on Tuesday nights. Not knowing this was just God's way of working something out and that our meeting in the middle was a divine appointment by God. The only reason why we met is that I am dyslexic, and I was in a special needs class. When it was time for them to sign me up for music class, the spots were filled for my grade level, and they had to put me in a category with upper-level students. So, two other students and I joined the music class with 7th graders, and I sat next to Sharae.

About 2012, Pastor Jason asked my ex-husband and I if we would like to be a part of Motivation Church. A church that God had given him a vision for. We were both young married couples in ministry with small churches. It just seemed right that we joined. Pastor Jason never got a call back regarding this offer.

Two years later, we divorced. A few years passed, and we are back at the top of this story. I was looking for a church home. I hadn't been stable in a ministry for the past few years. I'd just built a relationship with Pastor Jason and Pastor Sharae and would get several messages from them like, "Hey, you good? When are you coming by the church? We would love to see you." So one day, I decided to go, and on the way there, I prayed and asked God, "If this is the right place, show me a sign." I'm super big on asking God to show me a sign. Even though He can and will, I think He does it just to shut me up. I'll never forget it. It was like yesterday; it's still fresh in my mind.

Pastor Jason was preaching, and all I could see around him was that box. I saw the same box around me seven years ago in my old ministry before my divorce. I couldn't hear anything he was saying. All I could see was him punching and kicking the box from the inside until the glass shattered. There was such a freeness within him that showed on the outside. I kept asking God for clarification about what this meant. God told me right there in service that this is the place that will help you get to your next level. The place that will allow you to grow into who you need to be. You are free here, and it's OK for you to be yourself.

I was completely overwhelmed and had to fight with God before every service. Every service after that, on my way there, I would ask God to send me a sign; it was always something. Super Bowl Sunday was when I finally joined the ministry. I called my spiritual mother, Pastor DiAnna Webster-Armstrong to get her approval even though she knew I'd been visiting the church. I wanted to make sure that I was being open and transparent. I wanted to ensure that everything I did was done in decently and order. She gave me her blessing and released me to go. I then sent Pastor Jason a message saying I was ready to become a member. This was the beginning of my dread loc journey. To symbolize my spiritual journey and the rediscovering of who I am and who God wants me to be in Him. I am such a proud Motivator. My church family, from the beginning, has always made me and my girls feel welcome and embraced me for who I am. I'm so grateful for Pastors Jason and Pastor Sharae. They have been outstanding leaders, great friends, and family.

Give, and it will be given to you. A good measure, pressed down, shaken together and running over, will be poured into your lap. For with the measure you use, it will be measured to you." Luke 6:38

8

"2nd Quarantine"

The Covid 19 season was crazy. So many people got sick and lost their lives. Everything was completely shut down. We worked from home for months, and nothing was as usual. We were in a new normal and had to figure things out day by day. Wearing a mask and gloves when we went to the grocery store and hand sanitizer was a must. Numbers were going up and down depending on the city, and the entire world was in uproar.

I got sick with the virus during its early stages. Thankfully, I only felt ill for about five days. So being in quarantine reminded me of when I was sick at the age of 11. I was all by myself and isolated from my family once again. I'm so grateful that I could be in my house and that my loved ones were OK. I just now have the opportunity to have one-on-one times with God again. I was now of the age where I knew God and had a relationship with him. I asked him to show me in this season which direction to go next in my life journey. I do my best with healthy eating, herbalism, and nutritionists; I've also started a small business making all-natural products.

The covid season was helpful for my family to get enriched with vitamins and nutrients without preservatives found in foods and juices . I taught my girls how to start a garden and make all-natural teas to help their bodies with whatever sickness they have. But when I got sick with the virus, God gave me a new idea for my product line. Juicing was easier to do when the world was shut down. I want to rest, travel and enjoy myself. I can make and store items with this product line, so the summer is for my break . It wouldn't be as much work as making juicesTrying to do it while working full time and taking care of my family wasn't happening, and the summer is my break. wouldn't be as much work as making juices all the time? Right before I got sick, I told God I needed a break. I do so much for everyone else, and I put myself last. I believe this was when God sat me down and said here is your break; get out of it as much as you can. The spiritual well-being of an intercessor is crucial. Rest is important. Without rest, you cannot fully answer God's call when needed. I had time to reflect, reboot and recharge for my next assignment.

> *"And we know that in all things God works for the good of those who love him, who[a] have been called according to his purpose." Romans 8:28*

9

"12 Hours of Prayer"

When I tell you, this has completely changed my life in so many different ways. I became one of the members of the prayer team at Motivation. When I first started going to the church, I asked Pastor Jason if we had a prayer team because prayer has become my thing. We didn't at the time, but he said something was in the works. So he had Jasmine Jones, our fearless team leader, lead the charge. He started with a group of us, in just a year later, we were grown. This has been a fantastic experience for me in my spiritual life. To be able to talk about prayer with other people that like talking about prayer is insane. I love that we can just come together, share what God has told us and our walk and journeys, and be able to pray at intercede on behalf of people that know God, need God, or are far from God.

Jasmine had allowed us to do the first 12-hour prayer at the church via zoom with Pastor John Hannah and several ministers worldwide. As the 12-hour prayer was approaching the week prior, I fasted for a week, and I remember that day. I walked for 2 hours before meeting up with Jasmine and her bringing me to the church. I was in worship all morning. I was walking and feeling the breeze, listening to music, singing, and allowing God to minister to my spirit. I got home, packed my bag, and started my journey to meet her.

Then we got to the church. As they started the service online, I laid out a blanket and some pillows at the altar. To pray for 12 hours is not an easy task, but when you commit to it and know that God has a greater calling for your life and I want to use you in a mighty way. There is nothing that could separate you from getting closer to God. I can go on and on about this service because it was life-changing, but the thing that stuck out to me the most from that day was the minister that was praying said God is going to lay some people on your heart that I am assigning to you. Your job is to pray for them, cover them, and pour into them. You be their help. Even when you're tired, and you will be, still press. That night God immediately put three people in my spirit. Three people with three completely different relationships with me. These people see God in three completely different ways.

I could feel their hurt, their disappointments; It was almost like I was inside them and could feel every burden they bore.

These are the people that I need to intercede on their behalf, and I need to pull on God for them. I often wanted to give up because I knew the burden was too heavy, hurting even me. Then God reminded me He never gave up on me, and you need to stand in a gap for them. Your burden was never too heavy for me. I counted every tear and covered you even when you didn't realize I was there. As much as I thought this process was for them. Later on, I realized this process was more for me. I had to learn to trust God through the process in a new way. However, I didn't know what He was doing. I just had to be obedient, and know my assignment was not over. God is up to something, and I'm trusting Him. Through this process, I realized that God gave me three different journeys to allow me to realize that it was not me that could save anyone only Him. I can't force God on anyone. I could leave them to Him, and if they don't believe, I have to be OK with that and willing to let them go regardless of my relationship with them.

> *"I planted the seed, Apollos watered it, but God has been making it grow. So neither the one who plants nor the one who waters is anything, but only God, who makes things grow. The one who plants and the one who waters have one purpose, and they will each be rewarded according to their*

own labor. For we are co-workers in God's service; you are God's field, God's building. By the grace God has given me, I laid a foundation as a wise builder, and someone else is building on it. But each one should build with care. For no one can lay any foundation other than the one already laid, which is Jesus Christ." 1 Corinthians 3:6-11 NIV

10

"That's Not My Name"

After my divorce, the judge didn't allow me to change my last name. I remember her telling me you were married for 12 years and had three children, so that's my name. I didn't question it at the time, and also I thought it was good to keep my last name for my girls. I just felt the transition would be easier for them if we all had the same name. For that reason, I thought I was doing the right thing when it was pertaining to my children, but as years passed, I realized the name was more of a hindrance for me than a help.

Holding on to something that didn't benefit me was weighing me down naturally and spiritually. After some time, I did not realize it, but usually, when people need to be fixed, you need to fix it. Different businesses or my child's school called me Mrs., and I will get highly offended, and I would correct them by saying no, I'm sorry it's not Mrs., but it's a miss. One day after me saying that God dropped in my spirit the question, "is it miss?" I paused, and after the conversation, I had one of my daily talks with God, and I said I'm getting so frustrated by people calling me Mrs. But that's not who I am anymore, and this needs to be changed.

So I started to have my name changed back to my maiden name. Then Covid hit, and I found out the court lost my paperwork and I had to submit it again. It was annoying because I submitted all my documentation, and whoever heard of a court losing someone's paperwork. So I went and filed again. The lady told me that I should be hearing something within 3 to 4 weeks, and I should be all set. After patiently waiting four weeks, four weeks turned into three months. I reached out to them again because every time I called them on time, no one would answer or give me a callback. So, in fact, on the day that I had to go back to court, I asked them what was going on with the process of my name change, and once again, she said to me unfortunately, we have no record of you submitting the paperwork for a name change you have to do it again. At this time, you can imagine my frustration.

I was so aggravated and couldn't understand what was happening, but God would show me in time.

I was told the same thing for 3 to 4 weeks, and you should receive something in the mail. I said OK and just prayed that everything went through successfully. Within a week, I received the actual document of my name change. It was like a weight lifted off of my shoulders. I didn't realize that something that helped you in one season would be a hindrance in another season.

As my church and I prepared to go to the *Propel and Excel* conference in Atlanta, Georgia and I got up to the ticket counter, the airport had no information on my ticket under my new name. Weeks before confirming the changes, they said I would be all set. After 20 minutes, they got everything squared away, and I could board the plane and said I should have no issues coming back. But to my surprise, I had the same problem on the way back, and they even had no record of me coming to Atlanta. It was so frustrating to me. I'm trying to understand now I'm out of state, and they have no record. Maybe this is ridiculous. As my Pastors stood with me and I explained the situation to them, God dropped in my spirit to tell them the difficulty of changing my name at the court. After 20 to 30 minutes, everything squared away, and I could go home. On the ride home from the airport, I started to pray and talk to God, and I wanted to understand and get clarity from the experience I just went through.

I was going to the Propel and Excel conference. God said I couldn't propel and excel if you are not authentic. How can you be elevated to a new place if you're not who I created you to be? As I started to cry, all of the stories made sense. The name had such a stronghold on my elevation, both naturally and spiritually, that I had to let it go to get to my new place in God.

We attach ourselves to things both willingly and unwillingly in ways that create yokes of bondage, and we don't even realize the severity of the hold. Search deep within yourself and see what things you could be yoked to, and do not even realize it. That very thing could hinder you from getting to your next level naturally and spiritually. Unforgiveness, anger, resentment, failed relationships, addictions, social life, work and making money, pride, your circle of friends, and a host of other things. What has you yoked? In what ways are you missing where God wants to bring you?

It's also so important to realize the people you have around you. If they're not sent to help you, what's their purpose? Sometimes God will send the most unlikely people to bless you. So keep your mind open. Don't shut everybody out. If it weren't for my friend explaining how he saw me still carrying my ex-husband's name, it would n't have opened my eyes to the understanding of what God was trying to show me in that season.

Returning to my maiden name, I felt a sense of power and completion. There's a sense of freedom and peace in my spirit now that I've never felt before. I believe that I am being elevated as Minister Tiffany Marshall because of my obedience. I truly believe this process couldn't have occurred with me still being in an old place. I had to shift to a new season. I had to completely free myself of everything ancient to enter a new season.

Your purpose in life {as an intercessor} is about much more than you. It's just as much about the people you're meant to serve. No one else is meant to help them but you. When you procrastinate on taking action to fully step into your purpose and live to your full potential, you keep those you're meant to serve to wait, too. - Jennifer Spor

11

"I'm Still Here"

After evaluating my life, it's great to say that I'm still here, and God still has much more in store for me. He's just getting started. Everything has not been perfect. I have not been perfect, but I serve a perfect God. The more I listen to him, the more I'm obedient, and He opens doors for me and makes ways out of no way. Even as an intercessor with access to heaven's secrets and God's most profound thoughts, some things that happen in life may hurt for a season, but we need to remember if we stay in Christ, we always have a victory. Learn to dance in your storm, keep pushing, fight like hell no matter the situation, and remember that God always has your back as long as you're working with Him.

I've learned many life lessons, but the biggest lesson is always to Remain faithful to God. I pray that these words and my testimonies have been able to uplift you, spark a fire in you and help to push you to your next level. Stay faithful, obedient, and humble yourself to God.

> *"But Samuel replied, "What is more pleasing to the Lord: your burnt offerings and sacrifices or your obedience to his voice? Listen! Obedience is better than sacrifice, and submission is better than offering the fat of rams." 1 Samuel 15:22 NLT*

> *The apostle Matthew recorded the words of Jesus in chapter eleven when Jesus said, "The kingdom of God suffers violence, and the violent take it by force!" The revelation of this Scripture is the quintessential order experienced by God's elect as they seek God's Kingdom and His righteousness." Matthew 11:12*

About The Author

Tiffany J. Marshall is a native Bostonian who has been serving Boston communities for the past 20+ years. She spent her childhood years growing up in Dorchester and Mattapan, Massachusetts. She's the mother of three beautiful daughters, Tyanna, Kayla, and Jessica Young.

Tiffany has volunteered her time with several different non-profit organizations. She has 20 years of experience in dance, fitness, athletics, and health, and wellness. She is a Certified Zumba instructor and the owner of *L.I.F.E.* (Living in full Empowerment) *617* and *Nectar Lab Boston*, natural juices and products. She's a Hospice Certified Volunteer and an alumnus of the Boston Renegades Women's Tackle Football team. Tiffany has coached youth flag and men's semi-pro football and is a member and leader at Motivation Church in Randolph, Massachusetts.

Additionally, Tiffany is a member of the Community Advisory Board for Go Fresh; a program designed to give groceries to black residents of Boston to stop hypertension and her and the girls are also volunteers at Fair Foods. This program provides healthy produce to low-income families in the Boston Area for residents and first year college students attending General study's at Fisher college in Boston, Massachusetts.

Contact Information

For more information on booking, training or workshops feel free to contact:

Tiffany J. Marshall

Email: tjm.theauthor@gmail.com

Facebook: Author Tiffany J. Marshall

Phone: 857-256-1016

I would love to hear from you!

To order additional copies of this book:

www.amazon.com

www.barnesandnoble.com

Made in the USA
Middletown, DE
20 November 2025

22276938R10038